BRITAIN
AS SHE IS
VISIT

1st N.

£1-50 ~~~~ So♪
repcg

7/11

BRITAIN
AS SHE IS
VISIT

Paul Jennings

M & J HOBBS

MICHAEL JOSEPH

First published in Great Britain by
M & J HOBBS and MICHAEL JOSEPH LTD
52 Bedford Square, London WC1B 3EF
1976

ISBN 0 7181 1547 3

Set and printed in Great Britain by
Hollen Street Press Ltd at Slough
and bound by James Burn at Esher, Surrey

CONTENTS

ACKNOWLEDGEMENTS

Illustrations 9, 12, 18, 24, 26, 28, 30, 32, 34, 36, 38, 40, 47, 81, 100, 101, and 108 appear by permission of the Illustrated London News and Sketch Limited; and those on pages 16, 20, 42, 45, 49, 51, 52, 55, 59, 61, 64, 68, 72, 77, 85, 86, 90, 95, 97, and 105 are by permission of Radio Times Hulton Picture Library.

INTRODUCEMENT

Well come to England! Here you shall find the spirit of a nation ancient and with a march of ghosts from Stonehenge and the celtic dreams of druid (see the hurl of their stones on Salisburg Plain!), to the pulsing jet-Britannia and the spurting life that jumps in her efflorent cities; a modern bustling. Also, the calm and peace of her beautiful lands with bushy hedge; Kent hipfields, and many gardens of bloomer! Leafed Warwickshire! Bleary moors, when the curlews boom in the wind, and the larks song in the sky, as it was said by the famed poet, Percy Bt Sshelley! Or the famose Vale of Eves Ham known as the 'merry blossom time'!

You shall find tradition-moats, in every part castles and dainty thatched cottages which can all sing its historique of England; she is ancient democracy and parlimentsmother of all oldest. As their great poet Shakespeare himself did:—

This royal throne of kinks set in the silver tea

But you want a big information of her culture and 'bottles long ago', even for tourist who is coming already in a package for its vacancy. A hasty three hundred persons exalting from a Jambo Jet as much as luxury passenger; he can leaf the impression of Old England as a stamp on wax in his head, to know a little of her tale and how it was made. May be to visitors the patchwerk of her landmark Britain is all one loof, a wholemeat, you may seem it was a same people for the centuries. But not! Such would be a snarl of mistake. Perhaps too much is to err in the picture of English man of

7

Queen Victoria time with stiff upper lid and top hat, safe as Bank of England and his Empire, so like a marble!

But true is other. Here also was melting-pot of races. Here also came the inwader in successes! A stew of races to bubble already, before the Normal Conquest! Battle of Hastings is 1066, a veritable watermark in England. Now come the French Chevaliers which inject their darling manners in to the rough Saxons. So you may always see a pendule in the English character; bright and heavy, light and grave, warm and jellied. Even the Civil War (1644) was different! The Cavalier (laughing) and Roundhead (square).

So is the tongue fused, with Latin and French abstracts and Saxon-German a vulgar parlance of objects in *jug*, *thump*, *bag*, *smack*, *grub*, *hump*, *bump*, *lump*, *jump*, *pump*, *stump*, *dump*. Such became the majestic springs of her poets Keats and Yeats, Words Worth, Savage, Landor, and the vaulting top-spirit of Shakespeare himself.

So when it was formed into a nation of the English, this country stretched out its arms to the Globe. It was a nation of shipkeepers with her Navy (Royal); consider the exploits of sir Francis Drake who circumnavigated the world and abrased the Spanish Armada (1588). He was a prime of the Englands 'stiff upper lid'; when it is approach with bellowing sails, he ended a play of boule on the Hoe Plymouth (Devons), as cool as a cumcumber.

Such were First Elizabethans, a smashbuckling race of freelooters, like all people, but more. It was a glorious expanse behind the 'woolen walls' of her Navy. She marched with style into the civilty of science and art. In 17th century poets chanted with a metaphysique of sense and thought. Newton was father of gravity and initial of calculus-mathematic to start the modern brains. So in English empirical-

Guards have a famous precise walk.

mode, it was an apple banged on his head to perceive such a miracle.

In 18th century, Augustan, it becomes a prospering land of the country square with his port and huntings.

In this age also her colony America has flighted from its mother (1776) like a lusty weaning, but still to inherit the turdy soul of democracy. Also the Revolution (Industrial), the bronze clang and smoke of its steaming factory transport to the world's finish.

In 19th century *Tax Britannica* is ruling the sphere. And Queen Victoria shines with a glory over her Empire, a corset round the earth of all climates 'palm and pine', as, say, Rudyard Kipling. So you can see the proud hats of Beef Eaters in the Tower, her cathedrals, the fishports where amateur sailors 'mess about in boots', the pubs and mansions, the Bob (police man with no pistol), only a gentle truncheon, the Lord Major's procession; its little, by-wags, hooks and corner secrets, the broad acre under a doppeled sky, always a new wind to blow change. Well come to England!

INFORMATION

GENERAL

Here is hub of financial universe!

Money

Money in Britain is no longer to trouble the visitor as when they counted in dozen (it go back to the ancients heaping in Babylon and Sameria wich counted in twelve, such is their old! And still 24 hours in day).

But now she is jumping into modern with metric, you cannot have more to explain 240 pennys in £1, with slangy as 'bob' (shilling) and 'tenner' (sixpence), when visitor bother his pate and baffle in his purse for 'florin' and 'half-crown'. This old system is shovelled off.

TIPPING. You should tip such as taxicab driver 10 per cent or if you consume a meal but hist! only if the bill doesn't say SERVICE it is included. If your walter is smiling or does a graceful (he will be a Spaniard or Italic, the English waiter gives you a stern look and rumble under his breathing!) you can tip some more, he will not negate.

Hotels

In London and their cities, government subsides a £1000 for each bed constructed, the horizons foam with concrete and a hundred luxuries floating in the sky; Hilton, Inn on Park (Hyde), New Charlton, Garden Royal (Kensington) and many sumptuous edifices which circumcise the Town. And in the principle cities too, by the motorways are such, motel and Truss houses, also Post, a veritable chain.

Over more, now you can stay in an old coaching-inn or pub, typical of their old tradition with beam timbered full of

XVI century, its snug-bar with the twinklling brass pots and horse necklace on the chimneys, a firm cosy nest to soak in a 'pint of bitter'.

But it is not need to vomit out of your large purse to stop in a bed over the night; not for all is the grand lush of hotel firstclass with its palms. You can stay in a boarding-house. In, first at the sea-side, and all other places, you may see a carte BED & BREAKFAST. Here you can sleep and in the morning engorge a mighty breakfist, their tractional bacon and egg. It is a demi-pension sometimes with added EVENING MEAT, you may hate their three-coarse dinner with its Brown Windsor Soup, Yorkshire and Beef, Steam Jam Roll with Bustard.

If carte say VACANCIES there is an empty and you can come—it does not mean Landlady is out.

Food and Drinking

Yes! It is not to deny that England is inferior about the stomach. English have toured in strange lands and tested the global menu of exotics. They have tried the national plates, as Ladys Thigh and Wedding Soap in Turkey; in Greece fish soul, Salad of a Village, and Bowels Tomato Stew; in Spain, Squit in its own Juice; in Jugslavie, Gritty Balloons in Soup, Spit Balkan Fashion, a load of kitcheners bounty; the English men come home and hide such a menu in their drawers to remember.

But they had their light under a bush! You note here too some glory of their table, fat for a king also. Famous over the glob is their Roost Beef of Old England. Tourist must eat Boiled Beef and Carrot (Dumplings), Lancashire Hat Pot as also their great unical Steak and Kindey Pudding.

Regions differ also in their cooks. In Devon is a thick

cream (clott) which you may, but in Cornwall more clotted and dispatch to your pal (postal). All regions are some thing private in specials, and have a rebounding category of cheese; Double Gloucester, Blue Vinny, Station, Wensley-dale, Cheddar and Cheeshire itself. In Melton, porkpies, in Bakewell a Sweet Tart. You can go all through and find some dash to whet your belly, as Wiltshire Lordy Cake, Welsh Ratbit, Aylesbury Dick. And in Scotland Gridle Cake, Stones, Skelters, Auld Leckie and Immortal Hoggis.

An island lapped all round by the sea can pitch to the sky with its fish. It does'nt matter if you have Dover Sole, Herring Pickled, Crab, Tarboy, Puke, Lace, Trite, Salmon or White Bait in a tumbling dish with varnish, or if you want only a snick you may buy Fish and Chips in a News-paper, it is too fresh the same.

Yet we have not summed our list. Now in England are many China Men with Bamboo Shots, Sweet and Sour Noddles, Pork Bills and what you speak. Or India Curry, Pilau and Hot Foods. Or in each town an Italian smile in his porch and reckon his forefinger. And don't forget Aberdeen Steak House. Your tongue can be rubbed to an ecstatic taste of all in England.

Pubs

The pub is in the special way of socialist life and 'getto-gather' for a typical evening, or also Sunday lunch when they laugh on the paving. You can also in a lot eat food and lunch but not all ways.

Beer is *bitter* or *mild* or with blackhead Giunness, food for you. But you can not march in to breakfast in pub! It has a chain of law, time opening and closing, all different orders of legal to stop corrosion of children and virgins as in

The pub is not only for drink, it is for sociable cheer and eating.

lusty drinking-dens of old time, with a higgle of rules. So a tourist in Ealing (London, smooth belt) can find pub bang its door at 10.30 p.m., but hop to west end and sip till 11 p.m.

In babble of many speeches in a pub you must keep your ear marked for Landlord, he will cry in a stentor 'LAST ORDERS PLEASE', you can gulp it in a few minutes, then 'TIME PLEASE GENTLE MEN' and lights go out, you must evacuate.

Transport

Britain is a cobweb, an isle of radials germinating from the hub of London to every part, by all means. Road, railway, air, drains (as Grand Union, you can hire a boat for a peaceful voyage in the pastoral inland waterworks.)

If you wish to inter city there are many choiced days when British Rail are not struck and can take you in a whisk to Lands End, Peeble (Scotland), Brighton (its a Dome) Fish Gard (wales), York with its Monster and Shambles, a net of history to Romans, Edinburgh (Auld Leekie) and Stratford to see the Bird Shakespears play, (or what you like) and you can eat a bumper in their polite restaurant wagon.

If you desire to motor in the beauty, put your car on to drive it off at terminal, you will be fresh after sleeping on a confortable bank also.

By air you can radiate to Liverpool, Manchester, Gasglow, Birmingham, or hop to the Hebrides where they glide down to a beach smooth like a thistle's puff.

But if you should explode into the country side, like a vapid butterfly, and comb through its beautiful sites as you have chosen, that must be on the wheel. Take your luck

If train is late commuters can make a merry dance.

with a big heart, you will find the traffic can escape, soon you will wheeze through the fields like a born oyster!

In Europe average per dead of populace for each car is 4.2, from France 3.5, German 3.6 to Finland 5.8, (it is a snow-land); Britain is 4.1, but a crowded land, bump-to-bump. So you must furl your brows and have a pointed brain when you drive.

Here are some hopeful advice

. Britain has a proper certified mode in the drive on the *left*, (sinister) side.

. Rule at the Round About is attend the gentleman on your right, he is the Prior.

. Pedestrian (footmen) Beacon is an orange on a striped pale, and 'zebra' (stripe too) crossing (Belisha Bacon). Orange is alight. You must not halt in the dots. It is forbidden to hit Walker crossing there.

. Box Junction is a griddle (yellow) forbidden to come in if you cannot go out.

. Crossing Light. If you don't go it is red for you, and you do see little man green for pedestrian, you abide till little *red* Man and amber (yellow) winks to you (also peep peep in a whistle for blind colour), green after, you can now do if you don't hit one.

. Two Yellow Lines you can't stop for ever or at all.

. One Yellow Line you can stop when no one is working (off Peak).

. Dotted Yellow you must do what you have in 20 minutes.

. *Parking Metre* is 5p an hour.

It will find you a miracle how you can get into a peace with your car in Britain! The Motor Ways hum with the throbbing of jugger-naughts and racing commuters; but in

Piccadilly was hub of Empire with its memories of love (Eros).

a trinket you sidle off and it is an orchard or a smiling park, you amble under her booming trees while the birds tinkle, through villages, peaceful rivers and an ancient jumble of snoring towns with churches, the calm dust of century to wait the adventure of you. Happy droving!

Public Service

There are many generous public furnitures in the streets of Britain, as clocks, public conveniences often times under the ground free, but you must pay for soup and towel and telephone in a little glass shed. Same is for stamps-post, it is only by Post Office. Telephone shed is red everywhere except York ones in green.

To speak from a local box you can a whole minute for 2p or 10p—this is the coin you must have, another to continue, let it hand in your index to drop when you hear a sonning, *beep beep*.

When you start you can hear slightly but not always, your respondent, but only one or two syllables, you can't be safe it is the visited person, so have a great care you dial correct, when he is couped by the *beep* tone, you can't hear more till you dash your money in, it cant wait. It can only enter if you press in a practiced mode; many English themselve can not obtain it through such a tender device, some times you can see them bonk and rattle it with a curse! But if you clank and no reply, you can dial 100 if your money is gone and ask for a miss.

Shopping

Never was such an age for bargains if you visit Britain now when the £ (struggling) is a daunting change for the foreign, and there are a thousand dainty objects to brush your fancy.

More than British who live in it, because you can, find in London shops and often a card to tell you DUTY FREE if you wag your passport. Here you should gauge:—

. WHISKY. Hague Dimple, Teacher, Johnny, Walkers, here you can get a true noble juice from its source.

(. CASH MERE & TWIN SETS. A famous kind.)

. TWEED. Sometimes, its a beautiful roll, from Harris Island.

. MARKS & SPENCER. A veritable aim for the tourists. Shirt cloths, under cloths and all ladies, done by St Michael.

. HARROD. Is the unique of London, there you can buy it all from a grandpiano telescope or vast settle to a tiny Indian jampat (Food Hall). And electric vans.

. ANTIQUES. The soul of Britain who love old, in every place a thousand. Gloss warming pins, Chippen Dale and the quinted elegant 18th-century Commodes, Tall Boys, What Not, or Regent Candlesticks (Georgian) silver, a foaming choice.

. CHINA. A famous necessary. Old are Chelsea, Nail Sea, Stafford, Minton. Many are still, you can prefer the witty frames of Wedgewood, Royal Doulton Derby, and a lot.

. JAGUAR CAR XJ 12. Solid leather and wood in the face, yet a smooth tiger lark in its motor.

But you must choose. We can say it will pleasure your nose in our shops.

LONDON

Big Ben booms a national time.

What an occasion for the sighting tourist to spread his soul in London 'flower of cuties all' as their poet named! Here you must start, to see the fizz of history and life, the equator of the world's longitude pass through its roaring stomach, you can see the live zero at Greenwich (meantime).

Or you may stroll by bloomers in the greened flor-parks or in emnbankment of the river, hear a nice music from a band of soldiers.

London pervolves with a stout string of the past in her modern traffic, and many old coats bring a dash to the street, as Chelsea Pensioner old soldiers from classed Hospital, by the Thames.

Till, you come to the Square Male (City), and here other coats with a top hat, it is the Messenger of the Bank of England, hot feet with a new rate! Now you are in the old ghost where the Romans camped Londimium. Many persons come after 2000 years to 'bulls and beads' market on the Stock Exchange at this same place!

It was burnt in 1666; you can see the monumental of its fire. So the gable-end of Elizabethan domicile and her wood house perished, and a novelty of globed churches came by Sir Christopher Wren. First of this marbled zeal is the Dome of St Paul, a majestic to fit the state with some big forms of festal splendid.

The Tower of Norman Williams is the bloody fortress of London. Its stores exhale a vast history. What a scoop of legend you may impast here when you see the Yeomen of the Guard and the Crown Jewel, the grim of rack and thumb-

Each Beef Eater at Tower of London must have a pike.

screw, the 'Tractor's Gate' where many famous came and lost their head! There are ravers, a bird which fly and trot there; it will not go till England is dead, so you must rush to heed it.

Sometimes it is a nation's pin point, when a royal tie is crowned or married, and the bells jingle their mighty tabulation, the gins crash to salute and the people laugh in the waving streets.

Neighbourly is the Old Mother of Parliament, where Big Ben strike his horal boom on the Thames, always a light when its House is sitting. But you can mark a gentil smoothness in their debate; the minor part is called lower, which is not under, but equal.

Art Galleries

Britain has a great focus of art, for history; before the Reform it was a glass story in the window, and many triptyques. Then all was turned to the pleasure of a duke's house or a jolly framing for the boudoir, a rich collecting for privates. And you must not pay. The old authority of government made this obliging (as in others lands), but such a heavy screech edited from every, they have dissolved such a stumble. Well come to their galleries free!

National Gallery

Like a hearth of the world with its stout pigeons and fountains, where the throng takes its camera by the Lion of Nelson (Land seer with monocle on his adjacent pile), also a dais for meetings of public masses, Trafalgar Square has a grand doorstep of National Gallery.

Here is a vista of galleries sprouting from noble stairs. Some time you can jump to see on its own wall a real famous

It is a smiling photograph of some American ladies come to debut at Buckingham Palace.

post card like 'The Hatwain' by Constable or *Lady as Virginal* (Vermeer).

Victory and Albert
Here is a mess of pulpits, with ceramic, as well as Chinese and a thousand curled table, and the charming vapours of Constable again; you could pass your life and ignore it! Here is a truly museum land, you are against to the standing balk of the others, as Science, a triumph of Engines, with the Racket of Stephenson, a coin will twiddle it, and Natural History with staff animals, many prehistorical, and aircraft also, some with big bones.

Tate Gallery
Here you see Whistler *Nocturne* and Bloke (the Michelangelo of English with his muscle God) also many Manet and Impressions and the *Sun Flowers* of Van Gogh, as well the beaming master of Seurat *Baignade*, bathing boys with little spots.

Wallace (Collection)
This is a trunk of ormolu, French ornated clocks, also Fragonard *Swinging Lady*, Frany Hals *Laughing Cavalier* and Reynold, as well as a lot.

Other museums too if you can divulge at Hampstead a wild in the streets with open bush you find *Ken Wood's* mansion in its park with a great self-portrait of Rembrandt, also Dulwich, National Maritime (Greenwich, a famous paint ceiling), Sloane Museum (Hogarth House) and many most, each a particular.

Covent, Garden Opera House is among some vegetable markets now gone away.

ENTERTAINMENT

All can taste well. You may impeach for what you like from splitting comedy of Brain Rix to Grand National Theater, where you can hear the star of Dame (Maggie Smith, Lord Oliver) or Aldwych to speak the mobled lines of his Shakespeare down to a little naughty for the Business Man, with *Oho Soho* and *Dirtest Shop in Calcutta (Oh!)* by Tynan-tease with real jumping nudes. Permissive stints are everywhere in the capital of gay.

Music and its friends

The Opera House of London is Covent Garden. It was a market, the cabbage twisped under your foot and the orange men shouted their barrows, when you could hear the immortal sounds. Champagne under the spankling chandelier in the interval of Mozart, Wagner etc. And Royal Ballet also, you can see Maggot Fountain and Nureyev and again often.

At Coliseum, in English, but the same. It was a little called Saddlers Well, now it has rebounded to a vast luxury plant, an out-house of culture and gives a table to exotics, because many foreign troops, Chinese acrobat or Suede Ballet visit.

Truly London is a vertiginous cloud for the melomane. There is an embracement of riches to make a salad of your head! With London Symphony, London, Philharmonic Symphony, New Philharmonic, St Martins, In the Fields, Royal Philharmonia, BBC Symphony, indeed a vast of orchestras every night.

Many times a week you can go. Royal Festival Hall is in a complex. It is concrete with Queen Elizabeth for small and Purcell for intimacy. Between the passages is a welcome

The Albert Hall is full inside and out.

concourse where the bent and twinkling can make their drinks with shiny chuckles.

Or there is a resounding jubilee to hear in the orbal figure of a vaste caved marble, a grand loop swigged with the embellished splendour of Victorian brick and cooked stone— the vibrating *Albert's Hall*. Here the trumpets dash, or you can hear a master requiem or Grand Mess with a thousand-chorus in this singing country of Halleluia. London, Philharmonia, New Philharmonic, London Symphony Choral, Royal, Philharmonia Choral, Bach Chorus, Gold, Smith, London Philharmonia Choir and many more, it is an English virtue. 'If a man has not music in his soup, let no such man be trusted,' said Shakespeare again.

At Albert's Hall, in July, August, September, are the notes *Promenade*, a valid sight of young people who wait in their sleeping bags for 'Last Prom' with a carnival. But such a breath of solemn makes them lovers; a boom and stomp of young thunder, as they chant *Rude Britannia*, not to ever forget!

London is a metro pageant, a human sparking, a dream to hop before your eye; Dr Johnson said, 'Sit! If a man is tired of London he is tired of life!' You are in a clustered heart where history dances, if you look anywhere and a chance can spurt; always some doings on.

But perhaps your mouth is stopped at such a flop of the possibles, if you have a loose hour you cannot think. So here are some traps you should know:—

Law Courts
Old Bailey, you can see Blinded Justice with her balance. Here a free spectacular. You can go in the publics Gallery and see the Law unroll itself. But attention, not to enter a

You can find bargains in some famous junk streets, Petticoat Lane and Portobello Road.

dry case, like the fingering of patents or a tax doddler caught in his boots! If you demand at the queue you will ensign, if it is a murder of passion, or slander (label), or mans laughter, when you can see the cup and thrush of the acid legal brain and nice scruple of the Judge 'seen to be done.'

Petticoat Lane

Here is a famous Sunday morning market. You can rumble here for knick-knocks and pick-up values of a thousand items, with the dram of life, when you see the Cockneys in pearled trousers and old traditions (cry) of *Watcher Coq* and *House Yer Father* cross and repart from each stall with a flaring gust.

The River (Thames)

'It glideth at its own sweet wall' wrote their poet Words-wroth, 'it is a silver cotton through.' You get on a little boat past Southwark and Shakespeares Glove Theatre (site), the Towel of London, under the bridge and the Isle of Dogs, and the busy cranks of world's commerce in the dock to Greenwich where a navy's heart throb. Or you can go up to the loofy banks of Richmond and the master-brickworks of Hampton Court with his sumptuous Stale-rooms and a mazed hedge. Or you can dislodge at:—

Kew Garden

It is a peak of botany. In spring a floss of lilac and rodod-hendron, in summer, a smashed heap of colour with beds to boil your eye and tumble your nose with their waft. In the hot-glass houses you will find an incandescent twinge of huge tropicals, a great bloom feast which leaves radiate through a carnival.

At Madame Tussaud's some famous wax deads.

Speakers' Corner
Here, a rambled tass of good natured bantam and repartee. England is the bed of free-speech, and it doesn't affect what they shout on this platform of Hydes Park; the burly police grind his ear of toleration; communist, fascist, flat earth or crockpot with a letter of doom, you can notice the traditional wit of the crowd with a cry of 'rhubarb' (rubbish).

Madam Tussaud
A magic necessity for all who visit, it is a 19th century waxwork totally. It is a bounding assembly of unreal persons, you must punch to see if they exist! Kings, queers, murderers; scientists, statesman, and other criminals in a real group, also an essential Chamber of Horribles, all can enjoy.

The Zoo
Across the spacial Regents-park, a famous location of beasts. The towny lion, bear, camel, snake, and monkey, you can see famous chumps tea party; all you can think, also an aquarium with a thousand striped and glucose fish, and a birds house with a waving geometry by Earl Snowden (Armstrong).

House of Parliament
It is pat luck what you find after the public queue. Under the frowning ghosts of Gladstone, Disreali, Churchill with their ancient tongues of marble and gold, it may bump you to see the Leaders Bench with their feet up the front, and snore while they probe a part of the Swine Fever Bill; or you may see a lovely Twenty Question Time, democracy in a happening. They do not buff another on the nose, you will see the English Understatement for Defence, as 'the *Right*,

The Changing of the Gourd, grand daily spectacle.

Honorable Gentleman, a too-faced twip.' It is a true cradle, the Brother of Parliaments, her self.

Changing of the Gourd

Here is the gelded past of romance! Every day like a flicker of marital dash, a traffic stop near Buckingham. The Horses jingle past and the band thrall your blood with many brasses. At Horse Guards 11 a.m., Buckingham Palace it is the footmen marching (11.30) but note if the Royal Flag is not on its pike then you must amend to St James Palace up the Mall. There you can see the celebrity guardsmen with the grand bearskins and scarlet, or Life Gurds with vast boots and plums in the wind on their changers, truly a vestige to tangle your spine!

Welcome to London! Have fur in their city!

A cockney tradition of pearls and some big breads in London.

GEOGRAPHICALS

Country is always near the town in Britain.

SOME GENERAL VISIBILITIES

England is a patch. When you digress in its air you can see everywhere its soil which is cultivating by deads.

You cannot find a rolling plain without hooks or a savage wood. You might think it was Middle Age, but only old hedges are from it; England was forked in those green parcels, like a checkboard in 18th Century; now it is a humane aspect of the land to see in every part a share dotty with trees where a spirit comes with gentle breath.

You should note the sharp specifics that each building is from its own spott. Cotswold is a faunced gold stone, you could image each house is some honey. In Northamps it is iron like that colour. In Eastern (Anglia) people live in flints, the same their church which beam in a hard sun like a casket. Shopshire and Chester, you glance a full moot of timber in their manors, black and white. Every place is a regional apex, of its own style and matters.

You can see a vast apothese of such region in her fountain of churches. England has a famous bead of all kinds. In the peaceful yards you can hear the wind moon through the yew trees and a post calme drops in your soul! It can help to assure four bases, then you can say what period it was, like a professor!

1. **Norman**

You can tell it has a strong groin and a round arch, its stems like a very sturdy tree with dogs tooth.

2. Early English
It was when Goths found a pointed arch which could throw up to an apex, very pure. You can see this style at Westminster Abbey and Salisbury. They say a buttress carries the thrush.

3. Decorated
In Fourteenth century, a lovely extrusion, like knitting, some times a rose in the middle, or Dear's Eye at Lincoln.

4. Perpendiculiar
In the Pest of 1350 Black Death many crafts fainted, and they constructed more simply. Ignoring Domes and curled forms. This way has a squat, windows are millioned with four centres. A famous type is St George Winds or College of King (Cambridge).

It could fill your vacances to make a cathedral-hop. They are a radius of history like a tree with its ringed years, you can see in a same building an early arch, after 200 years a wiser fun, vaulting, after that 18th century with their dropping allegories of grief—yet also a vastness to stop your breath, with its searing roof and grand wet face in the sunset.

England has an only sweet prize for her visitants in the Stately Homes. The Englishman's hope is his castle, but you can go in also! Sometimes it can be a palace with slate apartments, Orange, grand tufted stairs and superb art work. But its Noble Man is not a grand who can snuff at the ordinary, it is a democrat; you may see one in his short sleeves rolling the grass or making a hodnod with his pheasants, and you will find it is the Duke or Lard himself!

There is an old fashion in England for his family to live by the land of his own, he is not distant in the capital. The

The Verger of Wing makes a bang each year with Fenny Poppers, Buckinghamshire.

large houses have a domestic heat, you can smell the generations as they throb in the walls. Not a museum; but you can see a little rope across the private parts.

There are many scales to find grand or intimate. Blenheim Palace, is a lofty seat of the Duke of Marlborough, also Churchill grave. Chatsworth Derbyshire Peck district, is a noble chair for the Duke of Devonshire, some fluted ornaments of water ordered to roll down its elegant stairs.

Warwick Castle reverberates with its history in Caesar's Tower, Great Hall, Cedar Drawing Room, Green Drawing Roof and a hundred. Luton Hoo is the Werner treasury; at Woburn Abbey (Bedford) it is like an exposition of Easter hat shows, tea room and childrens devices to amuse, you can take the weight from your foot.

At Bath, Longleat you can snap loins safely in your car, also at Windsor Safari. Many other houses are an apex of local grandeur.

But there is a second row of such delighting places you can enter, more personal, where a yellow manor can bring you a past age as it dreamed among the old trees; Compton Wynyates, Polesden Lucy, a thousand welcome you with a musical roll of their names, which charm you with murmurs of a life.

Gardens

It is a prime visible as you roll through their ways, that each English man is a voted gardener. In summer the air is filled with a noise of lawn-movers. Here you will find carnation, salivas, begon, dahlia, pansy, daisies, gladoils, or superb bushes of buddlea—it can make an impressioned dash to your eyes.

If you can see from the street, it must stamp your mind

'Come in Number Seven, summer is over.' A traditional park.

what it is to find a thousand special gardens for exposition! Like the Stately Homes it can be all kinds. Classic and grand are at Hampton Court, Hat Field, Blenheim and some more palaces. In many it is more than a ploy of flowers and shurbs, it is a melodious rolling horizon of liquid, which their famous Capability Brown in 18th century has scarped the wood land like a natural foam with its ungent lines, a smooth and pastoral antithese to the formed polygones and diametrique of Versailles.

So as you pierce the warmed gardens in the smell of summer you will understand what is in the heaving soul of the people, then you can shake with them what is only British.

Now are some other uniques which you may hit on a weekend.

1. Cricket

You will see 13 men in white overall on a flat green, it is their only national game, the most idiomate of England sport. It is better to understand why England is sometimes slow and sometimes fast, a noble game of bat and bail which have past into Proverbs, 'Its not cricket Old Boy' (you have done a rubbish unsporting,) and 'play a straight bit' (to do a Gentlemans and not under your hand.)

Rules are following. Patch is 22 yards with popping crase 1 yard from Stumpen which batman guard from bowler. On each side, elevens.

But bowling side only on grass as follows. Wicketkeeper and ON side to right of batts, Slips (Golly, Point), Cover Mid-off or Fool (Silly Mad-On) or you can have Third Man. Other side of Feld (sinister of batsman unless he is lefthand, then all are changed round is Leg (Square Leg, Fine Shirt

Cricket is a national game played with bat and ball.

Leg, Long Lag, Pine Log; captain can move them about).

They must catch ball if batsman loft it into the sky, then a clapping will scatter round the scene and a murmur (cricket is not to shout like a football stadium, it is gentlemen!) 'WELL-HOLD SIR!' and 'OZWAT!' (appel). Bat man is out, you can see the next one podded up in pavillion, now he comes. So always nine waiters are there. Some chit to their wifes in deck chairs or sneezo a summer day till it's turn. So calm a game—but with dramatics also, the poet spoke:—

There's a breathless rush in the close tonight.

3. Folklore

You must come on a Britton's folklore by steal. It is not to trompet in a national dress with branded petticots and peasants in their local trousers, as you may see in Europe. With folklore you may find a sodden surprise in a hamlet.

Hist! You can hear the measured boots on the gravel while an old air (dance) come on the fuddle or accordion; it is the Morris Dangers, they are some huskies in white with their baldricks and gaiter by knees, also a Fool which prance on a Hobby, his own legs but to show a horse, and blip the bystander with his Bladder as jokings.

Yet such are not ploughmen or rustics to wave their handerchief and jangle of little balls as they stomp. Suddenly Leader cries HUPP! and there is eight swords he hold up in a lettice-work! They are often salesmen, or teachers with beard and glass. All can in Morris Dance.

Also in Helston Cornwall, is a Floral Dance called Furry.

Abbots Bormley (Staff) is a Horn dance you must go in August to see primal manifest of such, lost in the antique fog of past. All day long they do with antlers on their heads, a veritable hopping of deersmen as in the magic and power of neolith caves of Lascaux, to bond with the spells! Yet these are todays folk-men of Stafford!

Such a versing is in the vernal 'merry month of May' as their poet cant; then on the village-green a thousand times you can see the childs dance round the matpole with a

Visitors can 'take your partners please' in Cornwall.

Horn Dance at Abbots (Bromley) celebrated annually after Wakes Sunday.

criss of ribands to welcome the owl and cuckoo that twit in the bushes 'jig jug tu witta woo'.

Other folklores are not so gentle, such is football in the street of Atherston and Ashbourne (Derby) on Shove Tuesday. You can see it up and down Main Street, heaving and pushing in a battle; the shop-windows are plonked up with boards to ensure, but this nearly riot at last goes in the jolly pub and everyone can smile and drink at daysend.

At Shove Tuesday also in Only, Bucks, housewives ran a race for pancake.

So on Hunger Ford at Hacktide after Easter, the Tuttimen march them to the houses up a ladder to get a kiss from girl at bedroom and all scramble from a basket of oranges.

In Fenny Stratford are 'Fanny Poopers' who bang their little canons on their Green.

This is the folk not thinking to itself but, it sprang from the deep of the nation soul, it is a thousand instants you can enjoy in the normal if you are when ever.

4. Steam

You cannot see in any place of the world a better nostalgic and polish of steam engines than it is here. With the flighting puffs of their first iron steers which they invented, Britain was the clanking trumpet of moderns, the Industriel Revolution.

Now it is a vibrating of diesel and electricals, so you can be surprised in many fields when you stop for a sneck or come round a corner, and you hear a puffing noise or see the nice steam in the air, and soon an authorised veteran locomotive will clink by.

You think it is a dream but no. It is the Preserving Society. In every part of England, lovers meet to polish the cranks at week ends and operate down a sideline which they have restored with a keen spirit. Some are in an official place of beauty (spot) and are opened for tourists through a scenic bank of vistas, with voluntary parters and signal men in a shiny uniform with jolly buttons.

In England there are 300 steam locomotives owned by privates! Famous lines are:

BLUEBELL LINE of Sussex, Sheffield Park to Horsted Keynes. In spring you can sniff the christened flowers of its name with also the oiled steam.

SEVERN VALLEY of Bridgnorth Salop, a great pastoral sort to Kidderminster Works, by a centenary bridge along the lurching meadows.

DART VALLEY is in 'glorious Devon', from Buckfastleigh in a company of the stream to Totnes. Now you can steam a voyage from Paignton to Kings Wear mouth also by the same, and all the year.

NORTH YORKSHIRE is a splendid air in your face from the breezy moots, where Stephonson himself made an inclined plate.

These are a pick alone; tourist can get a Steam Map to show all locations of these charming irons.

It can fall that you see all such in a lucky afternoon, in the summer when every village sports in a fete; you can tell by the bunting and flag which flitters on the buildings. It is a monster Rally of Steam Tractors (thrashing), then you see the puffs of those living engines with the chaff and rumble of their lusty pistons. At the fiesta also may be a Carnival with its Beautiful Queen and her hangmaidens, or a very funny knob-knees contest with Flower Show. You

54

It is a Pan Cake race in Olney on Shove Tuesday.

can take a side kick in a tent or coconut sty, or Bawling for Pig, or see a crazy bashing on the greasepole, and Tug of War; so fill you off the beaten truck; wherever you pour, there will be a special waiting to make a quirk in your memory; well come to England, the land of eccentric.

THE SOUTH EAST

Here is the primal hump of Britain that coils to the sea under London, a first impression of the land if you transmit over the white cliff of Dover. Here came Romans marching on their stout legs, William Norman at *Hastings*, and St Augustin to make the convention of Angles into a church. It is all a sprightly verdant of hop-gardens 'garden of England' with many smug and costly towns in its gentile valles, an old settlement of peace.

You can see the path of middle-aged 'goon on pilgrimage' by a high path from Winchester to Canterbury. The poet Chaucer made a first poem of their bawdy pilgrims tales as they stop and start. *Canterbury* is its queen. Its towers smile on the streets with its noble Harry Bell Tower and a peaceful sprouting of gothic in its arches (crypt is norman), and pilgrim shrine of Thomas a Beckett, tomb of Orlando Gobbins and a traditional mastery of the choir. Also St Agustine's Abbey and St Martin (oldest in England) and many old sockets in the town.

A typical of the region is its weather boardinghouses a very old construction of white planks. Also oats-houses to make the germ of barley (malt) for their characteristic cups but now they are houses of stackbrokers.

It is a pleasant vale with some bracing humps at each side, the north Downs (Weald) and southdowns also a famous sheep. At north are *Box Hill* and *Leith*, you can walk on springs among the grassy bushes, and at Chantonburg Ring and Devil Dyke, a notable horizon of turf.

57

Midway Towns; Chatham, Rochester Gillingham are among steeps with ghosts of Dickens (Gods Hill) and many old sailors, it was a dockyard of Royal Navy when English 'ruled the waves', you can smell the air of those old tars.

Royal Tunbridge Well is a beautiful town with healthy water for lymphatics, nerves and fibrous disorders with elegant houses of Regent George IV on its green hills, and a noted road (The Panties).

Chartwell, the home of Winston Churchill. There is a vast spirit in its rooms, it is a likely that you can think he will come in to pick up the paint and brush among the authentic chairs of his life, also siren-boiler suit and the Great's hobby of bricks and a very ingenuous flow of lakes in the pearly gardens.

Kent has a bounty of historical House and Garden in its manors where lords and Gentlemen have settled their shiny old furniture, hair looms and grateful old pictures in a bounding of florals. *Knole* of Sackville-West has 365 rooms, like a calendar and a roomy park. *Sissinghurst* (Sackville West also, a lady gardener married Lord Nicoholson) has many compacted themes in its boxes, each a garden 'white' or 'cottage' or 'rose'. *Penshurst* is Sidney's place with his helmet and a smiling Italian lake.

Surrey is a county with two heads. It is a stripe of London itself, but you can be in the tufted clumps of its windys like Box Hill, *Leather Head* or eat you picnic under some peaceful bushes, where the birds troll in a clean wood land with a calm smashed lake at *Virginian Water*.

But richest is *Sussex*. It can surprise you in an hour from the vaulting metro to find this deep land with woods, dawns and an airy sea!

Here *Brighton* is an original. The sea bath was discovered

Beauty and the beach.

here in 18th century, and elegant sicks came to plonge in the brine and make a remarkable curved Pavillon for Prinny Regent (George IV) Indian outside and Chinese inside like a marvellous soap. You cannot believe till you see its onions and faces, a bulged exotic in the bluff ozone.

After railways *Brighton* was called London-by-the-Sea. It is a merry heap of nice houses and the popular eat of welks-vinegar from stall, bunting arcades and their flossy amusements with an essential pier which Britain made first, a laced iron where you can fish, eat, or enjoy a musical shop while the water slops and burbles under your feet.

It has a true calendar which offers a jumping life all the time, it does not lose its residents in the winter, and its theatre is a trying place for new plays. Old Cracks (veterans) cars go a race from London each year.

Rye is like the past kept in a jelly, on a hill with cobbler streets and every house antique with a balmy history. It has a lifted church with a famous clock which two chiming quarter boys.

Petworth is a notable mansion of Northumberland (Percy) built by the Lord of Somerset in a vast park with many old masters. The famous English Gainsborough stayed here, also William Turner, father of a delicate Impression of light; *Rain Steam and Speed and Fighting Temeraire* are a grand focus of the Gallery.

The cost of Sussex is crusted with many jaunty resorts fitted with plum hotels, golf, tennis and little calm tea rooms. *Hastings* has a smack of fish nets after its famous battle, also a noted Fairlight Glee (beauty spot). *Eastbourne* is a gentle reserve with an awful Cliff, Beachy Head.

Capital is *Lewes* with a prison and a tradition to burn the Pope in November (Old Custom) but now passed over.

Getting away from it all at the sea side.

It is a hop to *Glyndebourne* where you hear the throats of world-stars of opera in a well-tinged galaxy as they vibrate for a beautiful production in a good-class garden with wine and your own picnic if you like; it is a veritable mount of civilisation!

West is *Chichester* with a strong cathedral and yachts men, also a happy air with the prestige of its loved new theatre and a jolly Festival, after you can see lords and dames of the theatre in its intimate round.

Home Counties

The Home Counties are many pieces of solitude mixed with a bustle as you come to the contingent of London or perhaps a new Town, or a community centre and waking shops in a nice cement place where it was always, a field, or their old villages in a varigal pickle.

It is a spring in the mind of the visitor to imagine, he is in the same, little county of *Berkshire* on its down where some curvatures of naked grass swelp with a prehistoric grandeur against the sky or down to the white Horse Scenic Vale of *Want Age* (King Alfred born here), or the horse lads jackeying there galops in the dew at *Hungerford Lamborn* —yet also steaming biscuit factory in *Reading*, or the bumping traffic of *Old Windsor*, here it is bricked to London and you can see the jet planes bonk from its touching air port!

The river Thames is its silver thread which makes an old curving dream right through. You can get on a steamer through its houses and trees to Oxford, a fresh water cruise.

Windsor is a crusty jewel of the first tapestry; it is the largest occupants castle in the world, you can moze in a nectical volution of court yards, gatewags, triomph-arches, gardens, embellished statues and a hundred pompy swags of stone; also the Round Tower and a majestical skyline, and its upright Chapel with privileged tombs and the centre of Knights of The Gaiter with its lofty banner suspendered in the roof.

It is a hop on the same day to *Eton*, a very ancient school of Gentlemen where you can visit the paradox. It was funded by King, Henry VI in 1440 for 70 poors, but now it has more than 14000 rich with a special collar (but now not more) also a beautiful chapel. If they rot on the river in rowing boots they are 'Wet Boys', if they play foot ball (wall) game it is 'Dry Bods', another old tradition.

Then you can pass along the river like a secret in the back, with a gliding traffic of boat houses as you sail past the gardens of roses; it is Thames valley with typical houses, the roofs hang on its walls in their little holiday towns laced with wood-work. So is *Maidenhead* where elegants come and make a joyful night with a dance and some wines at its elegant hotel of Skandals.

Now the bushy banks jump down from their high-up, to *Henley*. It is a famous direct plane of water which makes a regatta of boats; here you see strong East Germans mingle with the Western strawberries and the cream, in a hearty melange of summer.

It is not a fiddle in your brain to do some miles to *Dorchester*—it has the same title as Dorset (Dorchester), this is another, where you can see a special abbey with a figurated window of Jessie Tree.

So you pass to *Oxford*, the 'City of Dreaming Spites', the most famous dark blue university. It has a weaving modern life also and many traffic can go in the Broad High Street, also adjacent a factory of Morris-Cowley. But you

An English sportive walk for the blood on Sunday.

can enter a hundred sudden quiets of the collages, a calm of square grass with study about.

Chief are Brassnose, All Souls (here special fellows who can teach nothing), Hereford, Jesus, Morton, Oriel, and Balloil, also a universe bookshop (Blackwall). One can blast the feet to see it all! And yet an extra museum (Ashmolean with very many antiques and a high form) and the Bodilean Library.

It is a marvellous convanged speculum of learneds in a corner, of mangled beauty in its chapels—perpendicular or blotted into a harmonious composited pill of classics by Wren, Hanksmoor or Indigo Jones.

Its other bank is *Bucks*, a land of leafs that the prime is beech and some hills coveted by these (Chiltern Hundreds). In its south you can find some beautiful banks. *Marlow* is a nested town by the river also, yet in these leafs you can find a wily past; at *Madmenham* (a false abbey) you can smell the air of grand old eccentric rakes. Sir Francis Dashwood (18th century) made a temple of sin to 'do what you will' also in a Ball on his church at *High Wycombe*.

Go by the ways in this land and must in some famous church yard songed by the poets. *Stoge Pokes* was an immortal, ebony of Gray,

> '*The lowing herd winds slowly*'.

Chalfont St Giles is the seat of Milton in his great epic of Paradise (Lost and Found) and at Olney another, Cowper wrote hymns and was mad.

You can sense a vast ancient in its tree. When you stand on a high bacon at *Irvinghoe* it is a division, you are looking down before your nose at a vale of famous Ducks (Aylesbury) and its little hidden pants, another land, the teeming valley of Thames and London are in your rear but you stand on an old other, Icknield Way is a road from wash before Romans into Berkshire, like a ghost with feet.

Hertfordshire also has two heads with its bottom in London, then it is a pass to the fields with houses in their woods. In a little trot you can span some history, if you go from *Stalbans* to *Hatfield*, it was the biggest nave three hundred feet! It is a square cathedral of their first martyr but you can find an elder in the next door *Verulamium*, a tested Roman city. It is a fount of notables which christened Francis Bacon (Novum Organum, it was the bleating of science) in a little church of St Michael, you can see him stoned asleep in a chair!

Now as you join *Hatfield* (next) you can think here is the propulsion of the nowadays as the vast jets wang over a field, it is de Havilland air craft original here—but also a gem of Palaces where Cecil Salisbury trunks through the page of history like some quick silver in a thread. Hatfield has a tree, Queen Elizabeth sat under it. Also Old Palace, you think you are in a madrigal till a jet wink its roar over you.

Hampshire is a special department of trees and the sea, there are many belvederes where you can see its tumbling horizon into a blue, with many pastoral cows dots in its meadows. Soon already you can snuff the oxone of the sea in its vast arboreal of the *New Forest*.

It is a habitude for 'new' to be Old in Britain, you may ensample it here! Such a great wood was granded by Norman King and other monarchs and is now a great wild, not only a vast ticket of beech and oaken; you can come out of its majestical wood in to an often beaming glad, or it is a large empty that you can see for miles. Do not jump yourself if your car makes a clang in the road; its is the cattlebang to keep the lovestock in its boundaries. Now you will see the vagrant horses (free) which guzzle your hand, also deers. In spring there is a raptural blazon of its famous bushes, rhoodendrons wich plummet by your ditch in a welcome phantasmagory.

The apical splendid of Hanshire is *Winchester*. It burts with old grand things, a college for Wykehamists and the flawning immensity of cathedral which sits in a dear valley, a surprise through its arches of the street, once their kings were drowned here. You see a mighty sandwich of style Norman Perp and a mote of tradition, at Holy Cross you can have bread and beer gifted (Wayfarers Dope).

It is a land of abbes and monsters, as *Romsey* and *Christchurch* which is already like a holy shed to breed by the sea.

Now you are at the 'silver sea', with its historique of navy and commerce you should visit *Portsmouth* craddle of navy and a fine old home of wooden walls of Britannia (Pompey) of Tars with its famous *Victory of Nelson*. In *Southampton* is bustling seapost of oceanic linens, you can see a Queen glide up the Solvent to the dock.

Yet it is a babys hop to some major touristical joys of seaside. Across the Solvent is visible a joyful island, *Wight* with a magic of Victoria with some innocent towns, *Alum Bay* (you can buy a marbled sweet made of sand), *Sandown*, *Shaklin*, *Fresh Water*, *Ryde*, *Cowes* a magnet of yachts for its regatta week, and a grand prospect of Noodles (rock).

Bournemouth! Pearl of the south! Vanting over the waft from Dorset pin-tree lands! Bournemouth Belle was a train. Here is balneic-station first glass, where you may bath in fairys brises, or daze in deck chair by the wave, or you may walk round the famose Chinks, as Branksome all beautys. Because of tribute to her nestling climat, many ageds dream to come here in the night of their life and re-tire themselves.

But life prances up and no resisting to all ages with dancing halls and joke-spectacle on a fat jetty, where you can fish for cad, hake, merly and other sea-dish. Also music can tinkle in your restful head from its noted orchester-municipal in a pavillon. Come to Bournemouth and love linger!

Wiltshire is a voluptuous desert of England. You can only fly off the wheel in a train where it dashes throught the waving fields and some bare up lands like a whale, but if you do a second along its nooked valleys of *Pewsey* with its famous White House itched in the hill, there is an element! It is where the strange old men lofted the topping stones of their famous gantry, Ring of *Stonehenge*. You must ramble in your brain at such a geometry of the sun's apogle, what an erection they made with their little tools. *Avebury* is bigger

Children twist their steps round the pole on May 1st.

but they are not all there. All over this you can scent the old neoliths where the harebells tinkle on a ridge and go like a sheep with their old feet before history!

It is now you drop down to a hamlet snoring in its fine old trees or an elegant handiworked park. You can find them living in a post-card at *Castle Combe* where a little stream mambles the street with a delicate bridge, or *Bradford on Avon* the same with some yellow Georgians.

You can swing in a total pendule in a few minutes from two pillars, the pagan of Stonehenge and the gantle spire of *Salisbury* cathedral, the Christian talks to it over a vast century. It is the most meadowed cathedral in its close leas which are framed in a notable execution of John Constable, artistic royal fellow of the 18th century.

Wiltshire is picketed with many Stately's. *Wilton House* of Inigo, Jones has famous cub rooms (30 feet each way) and a beautiful rug factory of its name. *Fonthill Abbey* was a ruin specially built by a famous mad, Backford, to relieve himself when his wife died (although he was a rich sod, it was a big eccentric of the age). *Longlet* is a great Elizabethan with windows and Chinese wall paper, chair of the Marquis of Bath, and now its park is a grand safari with open lions, monkeys and zebras crossing its grass.

The most famous you should visit and die like Naples in Wiltshire is *Stourhead* a delightful garden of Hoare and Capacity Brown with a bent water, with nymphs and a temple of Love and its beautiful Paladin bridge in a noble effusion of flowers, also a house with some ornated chairs.

Dorset is a naked beauty of its heath which made a proper air of destiny for Thomas Hardy our novelist, who exprimed the strong lust of the earth in Jude Obscure, till you come to its airy coast at *Studland*, *Lulworth Cave* and a little quiet.

THE WESTERN REGION

The Western County is a focus of the dream of Europe to expand in the ocean, when the famous exploders farmed out in their little boots to round the world. It is where merchant adventuress, Drake, and some stout buccanneers tumbled out into the unknown waves. At Plymouth you revere a stone where the Fathers invented America. As England makes a point at Landsend in the same moment and place she broads to the whole world. In this department with its old smell of tradition is the only name of a place with an exclamation in its very body, Westward HO! like a trumpet (now a golf course).

It has a rich custom and palate of food and all things. Devonshire is a beautiful sucking cream, you can send tin from Cornwall also to your friend. Somerset and Devon is a bulged land of apples to make a jolly cider to jolt the blood in your veins with a warm laugh.

It is a land with some great swept wilds, Dartmoor and Exeter you can see as a high far blue, some wide sandys as famous Torquay, Woolcomb or the little rocky towns where some old Celt saints made a legend in their beehives. Even many English did not know it!

Somerset is a rich mixed jam, like an example. You could not think it was the same land to have a nest of orchards and its advanced romatic ridges of Quantock (Men dip) and Exmoor, or to go from the opened commercial of Bristol to the grand classic of Bath, its great apothetic spa of 18th century when the elegants came to dangle their wit in its Pump Room (Georgian).

Wells is a gentle cathedral with an astronomy clock in the wall, and some moving horsemen to clank the hour. Its nave faces with a unical arch invert like an egg-timer, also you can see some educated swans ring a bell for their dinner.

There are many interesting geological fractions near it. *Wonkey Hole* is a marvellous sponged cave of miracles with some fantastic dripping. Also at *Cheddar George*, a grand and very noticed cut of lime stone.

Bristol is its capital of the west. It is a famous neat city of sailors, with the saying 'ship, shape and Bristol fashion.' There is a brick and upright university and a noted church Mary Radcliff. Also an iron ship of Great Britain called 'English', which is a famous item. As well you can note a charming fronted suburb of Clifton where a beautiful bride is suspended across George Avon (River).

Now it is a growing marine vista as the River Seven plump into its christened Bristol Chanel, a far blue becomes the hills of Wales as it goes back, and you can make an oscillation between the municipal sea at *Weston Super* and the grand mud with many amusements.

It is also coming *Exmoor*, a fine airy blast of heather. Here it is like many a district with a taste of books, a deposit of Lorna Doone, a famous romance of R. D. Blackmoore.

Now you are on the rim of 'glorious Devon' itself, a land with red soul in its fields and a grand dented coast on two sides soon you see immediately at *Lynton*, down by a subtle waterweight car to its shore of *Lynmouth* with a great drama of stones. It is a region of stairs in all these resorts—big as *Ilfracombe*, where gulls creak over its rockies. Here are many old fishermen's parts; as small as *Clovely*, a stone ladder

A busy scene in the harbour.

with fronged cottages which is in everybodys' heart.

But the most civilian coast of Devon is its south. You can proceed to a necklace, every place a bead. *Sidsmouth, Budleigh, Salterton, Exmouth*, and various, an essence of the sea in England and their classed resorts; you will see the bath dresses drying on the window's edge, the childs climb on a rock, the board-houses laying their tea and sauce-bottles after a happy day with the sands, where the father's trouser is up his leg at cricket; a genteel week with no care.

But this is not a unique class. On the other side, of its noble bag (Lyme) as you go to the south it is the most noted English Riveira, it moves the top of its column in *Torquay*. It is a rich town with cultured avenues, apartments and hotels of a premier's class nested among some palmy vegetables, tropical, and there is a blue sea with many smart boats, you can do it also at *Brixham*.

Plymouth is a grand of the Navy in an arm of nature, an ocean's bustle wheels in its streets with an odd quarter and historical victualling yard. You can stand on its winded Ho! and thrill your nose to think that Drake did not stop bowling his game at the peril. Later with a cold head he banged the Armade in its proud gallons.

Behind is granite covered with a heath the great windy *Dartmoor* which can vult to 2000 feet and some marvellous airs. You can track a pony or march, but you must take your foot with a little map, or you can fall into a bag of its mud.

Cornwall is a late mystery from some old tin men of Phonica, Roman and Bretton Folk (fishing); almost you hear mermaids on the rock in a sandy cave at Zennor head. It is stark with a beauty set on *Bodkin Moor*, also many old mines of tin and leaf, or a moon-land of the giant's white heaps of china clay (*St Austell*), then surprise you into a village nooding by its crook of the river like a dainty. *Polperro*, to example is a nice little fishy part, also *Megavissey*, and on the head land of *Tintagel* a Arthur King castle with a tremendous airs.

At *Helston* May 8 is a famous Funny Dance (it is a song 'the fidle, the flute, the big bass frum ALL together in the Floral Dance). All the parts where you go are separate, it is a people, till you come to the needle of *Lands End*, past the covering of a vast sea for the handy surf riders on its elegant beakers as they foam in the golden sand, or *St Ives* a painted colon of the little houses where artists pass often. At Lands End the wind blows your nose from the Atlantic, it is a car park on a ragged final cliff, the long waves dash their sprat on its shelf. It is the end of England.

THE MIDLANDS

In the mid-lands of England a great soul expires from its green which roll-up before your eyes. And we can advise; it has a pinnacle for tourist in Shakespeare land because it was an emperor's mind who summed the world.

You must go on a pointed way, you cannot visit without! But it will also enter your soul if you go away and maunder through its lanes to the secret village where you can be its only visitant.

But first is a pilgrimage and you must enjoy the bumting Stratford on his birthday, April 23 also saint George for Merry England, when some great ambassadors proceed to his tumb with leaves. You can admire its lonely gable and hear Royal Shakespeare Actors Theatre, a real temple which droops by the willows of the liquid Avon and his wife Ann Hathway Cottage you can buy a little china of it.

You will not think you are so near to the booming crank of industry. But if you make a short divertment through its trees and suckered fields, you must arrive to *Coventry*, a truly nub of commerce.

A noted junction of the times is here. It was an old city with a medieval and Lady Godiva, she rode in her nude to reduce the income tax which her husband Leofric, (an Earl) pumped from the poor. After the bomb of war it had a somptuous re-edificacioun for its famous new cathedral, in a splendid pink mess of sand stone, with a baptist window by Joan Piper, next to its old burnt fellow.

Below is Northamptonshire; there are some famous big

old houses and hedges which the squares and gentlemen can dash over the hunt with their red tails flying and a merry toot of the horn, and some foxes.

All this department is a cincture of malted yellow stone (iron) which beams with a majesty in the sun, it is the same in the joining Cotswold (Gloucester and Worcester), but here there are many local domestics where the rich middle-age wool men also made a glory in their churches. A famous master work of them is at *Fairford* with a big hell in the window, (Last Judgement).

It is a grand contrivance with nature. You think the houses are an orgasm of the ground with a local construction to make a thorough atmospheric. It is a diademe of shiny brown; *Bibury, Morton in the Marsh, Stop-on-the-World, Chipping Campden, Sodbury*, the same but different where you can reanimate your ghost with a restful tea in their rooms as the holyhocks niddle against the sleeping walls.

Now it is *Gloucester*, a bottom crossing of the Severe where Roman jumped into Wales and a casket of history. It's cathedral is a marvellous sample because you can see its growth like some marks, from Norman to its recent of arches.

Now to the north is a romantical melting of hills by the Severn and the Welsh Marshes. In Wye Valley are some Deans (hidden forests) with its medieval charters; on its river you will see very traditional old skinny boats (coracles).

The first hill is *Malvern*. On its forehead you can look to the mystical west rolling in the Black Mountains of Wales, at your west foot is a dainty spa with a named water to mend some grips in your stomach, you can see some nice fret of wood and iron in its hotels of a faded calm.

Next you turn to *Hertford* with some more hills and its

Football as it is anywhere, in all weather.

cathedral of the region. Here is a famous map of the world, a fantastical of 1300 with Jerusalem in its middle and a prescribed detail all about; such as dogs head men in Norway, we could fill our Guide with its hundred fabbles, but you must go away to see some noble arches of Hereford and a chained library, biggest in the world.

Now you will find some beautiful grand long humps—(*Long Mynd*, *Wrekin*) as you pass from some orchards to a naked grass where some sheep wail in the fresh air, and it is the ondulations of *Shropshire*.

In such a land, or next in Cheshire where its roaming cows make a named red cheese, you cannot think you are only a skip from the bumping factories of Birmingham and the Pottery place. But here is a special true of English which you can note; its Five Towns of Bursley, Hanley, Stoke, Trent and New Castle were noted by the spurting novels of Arnold Bennett, and in Nottingham you can see the little pothead town of miners which throb in some books of D. H. Laurence. It is because they can smell the lusty vegetation of such near humps and the shooting life of naturalism in the savage fields which are touching every town! It is never far to the wood of Lady Chatterly's Liver!

THE EAST

East is the open plate of England with many cracks and dents where blondes came from north with their long prows to rape in the village, today you can see the blue eyes and hair on their children. But now in the boiling centuries it has made some peaceful little towns and much links of churches, and cathedrals which are jumping from its fields and fun-lands like a jack-in-the-pox.

In 18th - 19th century it became a sleepy; its manors and halls snozzed in a forgotten rustic. Some little engineers are coming now with their factories, and its parts can bustle to Europe across the north Sea. But here you can smell a time before engines, when its towns were made of wool. It was always full of some very separate men in a quiet air.

Essex is a land of poles. South where the industry of docks goes up the river Thames into many dormitories, and here also Ford with the picturesque Girl Strikers of *Dagenham*. But in the north it is brushed by a large sky with some villages folded in, and a very fancied bulge of plaster (pargett) on their walled houses.

When you come out from London you are still there when the majestical *Epping Forest* sucks you in a still shadow. It has some huge glades where you can walk or horse on a mat of old leafs in a church of nature, and many grand forks.

Then presto it rolls to the open, with a hundred gentle farms. At *Dunmow* there is a church and an old costume, a piece of lard for a man and his wife who have not done a cross word for a year and a day (Dunmow Flith). Then you may float to some remote towns very English; *Saffron Walden*, *Twaxted* with illuminated churches. You can eat in a charming hostel and then visit a famous State Home, *Audrey End*, a twisted mansion with its metered turrets on a grand Brown lake.

On its other side are some very alive necks for sailors; Black Water, Crouch, Colne, and some famous muds. It has many seasides and each with the most sunshine tabulated. *Southend* is for jolly old men on a day (and wives) with a bounding and some huge fountains of amusement; its pier is a record, you must take a train on it.

The north bounds to some opposites. *Clacton* also has some large peoples fun, but you can forge by a typical pendulum of Britain a little way to *Frinton*, some good sand for Ladies and Gentlemen which make a holiday in its streets very sober.

Oldest is *Colchester* with a hunt of legend. It was a great place of the big queen Boadicea of battle with knifes on her axle, also Roman and Norman with a tremendous Keep (castle). Its natives in their local beds are some beautiful oysters, which you can month in its proper mouth.

Cambridges-hire

The delicates of beauty aspire from its flat, it is a hundred marvels in the town of its name where some great thought can tremble in its elegant stone. The most is Kings College, a perpendiclar with some noble volume and a hundred towers that roar into the sky, some very good fans in its roof, and a famous chore.

You can go down the River Backs, when the calm fields glide into it and pass. It is a place to dolly in the punt as you slide under some noteables as Bridge of Sighs (St Joans)

The traditional heralds are like beautiful playing cards with legs.

with a sweet plopping of drips from your pile. Trinity has a glory library by Sir Wren and some curving by Gibbon, it was the college of the Father (Newton) of Science.

Sometimes colleges are called Jesus, St John, Christ, Magdalen and other; Christian names like Clare, Corpus Christi. But now Cambridge (Cant) is a focussed module of science. Fitzwilliam (museum) has a winged pickle of art; it goes from salt pots to an elegant Gainsborough picture, *Mr & Mrs Andrews* in a field with Breughel.

Now you can find a second mirage, it is the beautiful cathedral of Ely which stands on the sky with reliques of Saint Ethelreda (once it was an Island of Eels of this name).

Suffolk

Here is a land bursting with churches. Its capitol is Burg St Edmund where you can amble in a park bowling green where it was a vast abbe of St Edmond (arrowed by Danes). Here some noble men sweared, to get Magna Carta; it was the birth of democracy for barons. *Lavenham* (compulsory to go) was made by a wooden merchant Thomas Spring; the town is a packet with a Guildhall and many ornamental dwellings of cloth men.

It is a glorious *Long Melford*, a perpendicular with a lily window. *Blythe Burgh* is a marsh cathedral with some smart white light and many delightful peg ends of fantasy on its benches. There some incredible roofs of hammer beats at *Mildenhall, Woopit, Needham, Market* and a lot. You should not divage from any, there is a tickle in every village! (*Denniston, Fressington, Denston, Freshfield, Denningfield;* also *Farmlingham* with a great castle of Bigot family and many more, like a bucket).

Then you must come to *East Bergholt*. Here is the ambience of our noted painter who invented the landscape, John Constable. You can see Flatfood Mill where the Hag Wain inspired birth, also Cornfield, Dedham Vale and many trees like his famous idea. You should do a little trot to *Kersey*, it is a post card with water in the street.

On its ocean many pebbles dash with the surf and there are some airy and heats with goose-bushes and a turf where some birds plank from the sea and moan in the sky, a paradise of nature (also golf link) till you come to *Aldeburgh*. Here is a famous town of opera (*Pete Grimes, Albert Hearing*) by Benjamin Britten; now there is a festival of him every year in its restful maltings in some beautiful mud and reeds at *Snape*.

Southwold is a silent gem of Victoria with some greens by the sea; and you can smell a capital froth in your nose, it is their famous beers.

Another town of Suffolk is mecca for horses with national Stud, also many famous races (Caesar Witch), this is *Newmarket*.

You can find also some eloquent rustic seats. *Heveningham Hall* with a marvellous rumbling inside of Wyatt, and his orangery, also a Brown Lake; *Melford Hall* with Hyde Park porcelain collected and, on its corner some admired pepper pots.

Norfolk
Here is a bosky regional of open partridges and peasants, so natural it has named a jacket! It is not a journey to another place, it lives alone. It is a bulge of England with many sedges to make its charactered roofs of 'Norfolk Reed'; also the most corny land (arable).

In its heart is a city like a small head, *Capital Norwich*.

Here you can imbue a medieval ghost from its cathedral, a grand Norman with a spine and towel in a majestic cross, also 32 more churches standing upright in a style. It has a prime castle, now it is a shopcase for her children of Norfolks-art.

There is an elegant circumference of streets for footmen and antiques that live there.

Norfolk has many divisions of Broad water; they were peat holes of neolithic kind, you can see his factory of flint at *Grims Graves*. The broads are *Hickling, Walsham, Barton, Wrexham* and a lot. It is a special vocation to hire a sailor at *Potter Higham;* you can live on it for a week or two. Lower the boom or jump up the flapping canvas to bellow in the wind, and tinkle slowly through the fields of water where you can see much wildness and birds to peace your soul!

Round its bending coast are some places for very quiet families on the sea, as *Sheringham, Hunstanton,* and *Cromer* with a famous lifebelt.

Lincolnshire

Is second largest department, cut into Fens, a very low part with dykes, and Wilds, a high edge with many spaces. It has a very interesting resemblance of names, you can think they all end in *by; Wragby, Saltfleetby, Spilby, Bealsby, Candlesby, Grumsby, Harby, Slothby* and a lot. In *Somersby* you must drink the spirit of our laurel poet Alfred Lord, Tennyson with a loved output; *Lacksley Hall, Enoch, Arden, Idyll of King* and the famous *In Memoriam* and '*Come into the garden.*'

At its top is Lincoln city very old, Lindum Colony of the Romans, and a most ignited noble cathedral, you can see its

You can walk to many beautiful dents in the coast.

It is called Beating the Bounds. The burgess doesn't know the name of a copse en route, so they hoist him while the guide Cornelius Edwards spells out the name with a stick.

sky line when you are far, like a prayer with three towers. It is a true stone gem with a famous Angel Choir in a forest of early English and a goth of florate animals and grotesque also; it has a nominated Devil, Lincoln Imp. In the town is an altogether of many relics; Jews House, Aarons house, oldest with a person inside in England.

If it was not Linconshire you would think St Botlophs in *Boston* was their cathedral! Its tower is a famous Stamp, a grand decorated and some marvellous evolved figures under the stalls. It is famous for Americans. You can see the cells of Fathers (invented USA) from a nest of puritans who founds its name in Masachussets.

There are also some very other dainty small towns all the same especially, *Stamford* where every street bumps your eye.

It is near the summit of England's Elizabeth houses; *Burghley* (Cecil) with a room called heaven of Verrio, 700 art objects, a rose garden and some nice plotting of Brown (Capability).

You could pass it all in the East for a week. It is a sole land with many beautiful congregations which will spell you mind.

THE NORTH EAST

Above Humber and Mersey River you will find some very rocky people; they are like crags itself in the grass. It is the north, also with many pastorals but the first English industry, is smoking also out of its chimney here.

Now is to notice a paradox, there was a teeming of opposites. In the 'wonkshop of the world' the hard mechanics lost their souls in a fine music with some famous choirs and art. The millers of Hudderfield did their Messiah a thousand times each year, each one better, also in Vienna, Lisbon and the world. The work men in their clogs became a real painting by Lowry of them.

The breath of its high landed moors is in their heart, and from a cheap small street you can see the beaming sky line which reckons.

Yorkshire

The grand county like a biggest shape, east and west Ridings below and North above them. The city of York is like a majestical spider of this web where arms can radiate, a famous joint. It was Eboracum of Roman. It is queened by the goth admiration of its minster cathedral with three towers and five sisters, a famous widow. Here you can see all excrescents of style as it was made, a jewel of European civil. In the city you must promenade on the wall and see the noted butcher walk of old time Shambler.

It is a distinction of many cuts made by rivers out of those grand messes of land, the Dales, some beautiful dents which can roll to your eye's pleasure.

Then you must go to *Haworth* where the spirits of Bronte, Heath Cliff and Jane Eye are blasted on the wind, you can imbibe the element in such a high wild air of it.

Here is a finish of commercials and you are in the strong pleasantry of a truly tourist country at *Harrogate Spa*. It was an elegant mineral water for sicks in 18th century, now a favoured nest of conferencers. Its Pomp Room is today a museum leading to another, *Nidderdale* for walkers with lust; or down it, to *Knaresborough* like a pretty drama with a bridge and castle and the oldest chemist in England.

In West Riding also another abundant cathedral of *Ripon* timely english, with a strong woodwork of animals. Near is a well known empty, Cistercian old monastery of *Fountains* in a subtle valley where you can throw some centuries away and some fine trouts.

In *East Riding* are many grand flats and it should not arrive to annoy you with an overall majority of holy stone in this part that you do not visit *Beverley Minister*, a lovely prize with Percy Shrine and 68 misercords, a record.

Soon an ozone from the sea will establish your head and you may vert to the typical resort of *Bridlington* (also a famous ecclesiastical with a Decorated Perch) with some fishing smacks and air. It is behind the great nose of York-shire, *Flanborough Head* with a vast colon of savage birds as crake, gullmot, puffwing, reds, killwake and a lot, where the stern froth of the North Sea dash their trumpets on its hardy bottom.

Then it is a tumbled climax, the heaved majestics of North Riding with two massives. East of it is North Yorks moor, a large aspect of lovely sweeps which plunge in the sea.

Workers can look out to model beauty in a park.

West is another altitude with a vast of Fells (moors), Lows (very high), and all swirl to join to Lake District and almost Irish Sea.

Before you hoist your sack to the vigor of the N. Yorks Moor you should stop in some near littles, for the nicely Palace of *Castle Howard*, even York men say it is big! It is a grand domed feature with a superb marble hell and some high costed pictures of Tinterotto, Caneletti and a thousand; also a Temple of Four Wines and after it you will be in its Mousoleum.

On the moors you can pick their heart if you tramp by you own feet where the heather burbles in the song of its only birds. You can see nothing for some miles, or you will jump to see some giants balls on the edge; it is Early Warming Radar at *Fylingdale*.

Whitby is a charming self port with some special old boats called cobbles, and a holed abbey on a hill. It is all saintly ground of a synod in 664 when the Irish Easter was changed into Roman (christian).

On its other massif there are not to count some more sublime ondulations like *Wensleydale*, also a cheese. You can wonder to many wild rollings with their grey stone wall and stout villages; *Kirkby Lonsdale* under, or *Dent* on top as ensample, like a placed gem in its upland. It is a National Part with an official and certified beauty.

Durham & Northumbland

There are big coatfields and a bush of industry between the middle spin of mountains (Pennies-Cheviot) and the sea, but it is all the time approching a cinctured open on the front with Scotland, a wild ram part. The named city of Durham is a grand hard thing of Norman. They made a rebel against William Conqueror and he must do it again! Then they built a record Norman cathedral with many turned solid pillars, which smiles and frowns on the riverwear, also an old university and some music. All ready the last English fort against wild Picks and Scots from above, now you come to some links of them from the coast. It is a climb up the castles of *Warkworth* (very dramatical), *Bambergh* which falls into the sea and *Alnwick*, a strong hole of Percy and his old family. It has some history with a bloody old smell but then it was civiled in the 18th century; now you can see its heaved grim sides but also some elegance, in by Adam and out by Brown.

Soon it is *Hadrian's Wall*, edge of Roman world, you must go to China to see another! But it starts near Newcastle and spreads its huge fling near Carlisle.

You can stand like a sentry starting at the wild fog where the north bounders live, but you can today see only beautiful areas (Northumbrelland is still in England, what you see).

Here is a fair end to England and its pieces of several kind, its empty fields and jumping towns (you can see here at *Stocktown* world's first railway, it was also home of John Walker, invented matches); it is a truly mixed pudding of life.

THE NORTH WEST

If you can only make one go from your sejour it will fall out to you in a coincident that the motorway is like a spine of the brain in the body of England, the technic has followed nature! But it is not to ascend M_1 to its peak, you can only end in Leeds (Yorks). You must vert to left on M6, you can pass *Birmingham* on Spaghetti (junction) and you will pass to the other romatic side of water. Already you can see some nodules in:—

Staffordshire

It has a world making of pots and chinas (wedgewood) also sanitary earth (Armitage ware) but you can turn to the cathedral of *Lichfield* and its spires Ladles of the Vale and berth of Doctor Johnson.

Cheshire

Now on left of M6 is a country of smiling cat and cheese. It is a reduction of England herself because it also has some grand constructed parts of Queen Victoria, at *Runcorn* some bridges of Manchester Shop Canal with chemicals on its water, at *Crew* a big meeting of railways in a gang. But in its gentle rural parts you will find many delightful residences of executioners from Manchester also some special moat houses.

Derbyshire

On right of M6 is a grand geological exhibition up and

down. Beneath, are many coves with stalagtites, it is a center of hot-poling sport, also a noted gemm of the place called Blue Jean which they bruff into necklaces clicks and ornamentals at such a place as:—

Castleton

Above its ground it is the start of a long Pennine Chair with its famous Peat (National Park). You can start in the south with some beautiful dates; *Donedale* where a celebrate fish writer Isaac Walton threw his flies, and *Monsal* where a pure water tinkle in the breast of hills.

Also is *Bakewell*, a resort with tarts. In this land is the spout of a sole custom to dress well. They do it at *Tideswell*, *Tissington Yougreave* and a lot. On a day, they put a big face of clay by their well and post some pictures of the Bible to it with flower-pedals; very historical.

But its top is *Chatsworth*, a prime of England, a mamoral cluster by the Lord of Devonshire. It is a place in some swerving hills very soft to find such elegant stone there. You can see its Pained Hall, and some very rich chinas. Outside it some majestical ploys of water which can squirt their beautiful drops in a pleasing arrangement.

Lancashire

Now you must be in the Grand County and Duchess of Lancaster. You can read its tumbled history in Wars of Shakespeare where they carried a Red Rose against the Whites of Yorkshire. Henry VI was their king not strong, a saint and sometimes mad with a strong wife Margaret. She defeated Warwick (Yorks) at Wakefield (Yorks), then Edward (III, Yorks) defeated her at Tonton (Yorks), when Warwick (Yorks) joined the others (Lancs) and was defeated

Relaxing by the sea at Blackpool.

at Barnet (Herts) by Edward, then Richmond (Surrey) defeats Richard (Yorks) at Bosworth (Leicester) in 1485 (all out).

They can still fight it at cricket but now Lancashire became an architect of industry. On the right of M6 is its largest of *Manchester* built on cotton with some fine culture (free library and trade), BBC and university and a bust life. On its left is *Liverpool* with some big decks and a liverly air. It has a jumping people called Souses who unveiled the Beetles (pop fundsmen) in a cellar, also some new cathedrals. The Catholic is a wonderful tin of blue and glass, like a lantern; Anglican is a pomped bulk of traditions gothical.

Here soon now is *Blackpool*, like a vast made cake of jollity!

You can galop donkeys on its blustered sand but its climate does not matter a fog! It is a factory of human delights made, you can enjoy it if it is passing with rain, even. Chief is a famous Tower like Eifel with a ballroom and a pier where many great comicals of England are discovered, and an infinite promenade where some opened trams clink past its ornamented flower, with vast lighting and a dash of popular life which roars and hums. Further is *Morecambe* with an empty bag of huge sand and some prawns, very quiet.

Cumbria
Welcome to the Land of water, an aquatical paradise to moist the image of its poet, William Wordsthrow and his Colridge and many more, you can see their lovely places at *Rydal*, and a lot! Look, from the slopes of a Fall and also plunge a lake in *Conniston; Ullwater*, and you may find a little tarn to spit yourself. You can do anything!

Hype Hank and Buttock, a well-known ancient style of wrestling.

But our visitant should note to march with stern Boots and firm raincot, for here often the storm can quickly pump out of a jolly sky. Yet this sudden wet is glory! After it you will see the rainbog-iris broach the air with an ether's laugh, and all is to wizard the look. So is not other, why Wordsworth (also Stump Collector in West Morland) mused in Rydal-mont

I wondered lovely, as a clod.

You should also see a wrestling-feast of the brawn men of Cumberland in a special style, where they also run up fells, and you can see the indigent shepherds and farmers of this part with their dogs for sheep in a test.

The cole of its nodal system is *Kewsick* a very delicate laced town in a web of hills by Derwent Water. You can go east to Ullswater, West to Wast Ennerdal Crummock and a lot. From Waste Vale you can go in a pictured very small railway of Eskdale to *Ravenglass*, it will seem like a tot with some open carts.

Cumbria is a poem which you can live till you come to *Carlisle* over the Shape Fell; it was a prawn between England and Scotch and Bonnie Price (Charlie), with a pulse of history in its red stone to be the finish of England, it is worth it!

SCOTLAND

'Scotts land' is another book of itself, its author invented romantic history in a novel. It is a colour of flaring tartans, Steward, Camp, Bell, Angus, Gordon, Teachers, Mac-Donald, and Black and White. Habitants can skirt to the pipes with some sporran-featers, or the torch cressers sputtle in the grim stone of their old castles like Macbeth, a back-clot of too much history.

It capitals of *Edimbourg* is Athens, of north, also where there is a cement; it is from turbulent street of Royal Mile and its toured castle and John Knox house (a big elder), Holywood Palace, St Giles Cathedrel with its famous Happening (Jenny Goddes threw a stoop), to an elegant formation of Hanover, its New Town with some fine porticled squares, and a Festival invented by its Scotch native Rudolf Bing to form a crux of operas and apical musicians from the world each year in some little church halls, with a mad fringe.

But you will waste a treasure to go there and not stop somewhere else in the Lowlands. There are some purple moods and you can sport with your gun and rod in its clean burns which puke over some stones, or find a comfort town like *Pebbles* nesting on tweed.

On west it is very infrequent. But there are secrets in their dented bats of coast where you can relay your self in a pleasing calm town like *Krickudbigth* (Stewartry) or *Gatehorse of Fleet* or *Newton* (*Stewart*); even Scots do not know it is there!

The Queen and her people are focussed on something out-door, a sheep-cutter's competition.

Now you cannot avoid *Galsgow*, it is a grand focus to north and south of four million in a thumping heart of the land with all ages, it clangs with the red hot strikers and rivets in their boatyard of Clyde where some giant Queens and a lot were lunched. Its famous Street is Sauciehall, also a noted Art Gallery and university and a lot.

Loch Lomond is a starter to the marvelled crag inlets and bent coast of her west, the High Lands and Islands. You can daze on a nice boat up through *Kyles of But* and *Tarbert*, or go in an intimate aircraft which glides to a small grass or some sand, to find many isles empty with the life of simple crafters.

Inner Hebrides are *Staff*, *Muck*, *Egg*, *Sky*, *Mill*, *Jury*, *Isly* and a hundred littles with an admired vacancy where the vistant stands on its seaweed to see the grey seats jump there in its blue water full of leg ends, you can always hear some Mendelsshon of Fingal Cave creep in your ear! Outer are *Barra*, *Ben*, *Becula*, *Lewis Harris* and some more. You can buy a lovely tweed where they die with vegetables. Some are vacant, some have a big prosperity of their famous Whisky. And if you come you must go, to some famous gardens at Inveraray sub-tropical, a miracle of Golf Stream, which flow nearby.

From *Oban* with a delicate port you can traverse to *Foot William* and burst your soul in the awful Grumpians, very splendid. The main is *Ben Nevis*. It is the west end (south) of a noted cut of water all gone to *Inverness* east (north), sometimes it is the artful Celadonian Canal, sometimes it is a Loch (Ness) with its famous invisible Monster. Below it the Caingoom Mountains in a stupendous wild. Above it some more of Ross Comarty and Sutherland till you come to its place where you tip John O. Groats.

Visits in the summer, can see some Games where they shot their traditions; the note of the bogpipes with an elegant (traditional) footsome style of dancing called Highland Fling, Reeks, Jigs, and some humming Garlic with no words in the lips, a special called mouth Music; also the unique thing of this land, Tossing the Caper when some lads can hurl a big tree in the air!

Then as you come down you will see a famous town of cake (*Dundee*). You can find a bloody story everywhere (as *Glencoe*) which thrums in all their complaining ballads.

Now you finish in the country of Fife with a primitive famous baptistery of golf which they invented at *St Andrews*, it is their patent saint; the Royal and ancient with its famous Four Curses (Old, New, Even and Jubile). Its other beautiful sight is an old philosphical University, you will remember the scarlet goons in the wind by this grey sea and stone in a romantical set.

Now you are by the waters of the Frith of Froth, soon you can come to its grand bridge and back to *Edinburgh* and your head can be singing after such a Grand Tout of Scotland!

WALES

Here on the door stop of England is a region of poets who chant in their mountains with high airs of their notion. It is full of musty legends which tremble in its air very romantic because they are Celt (high checkbones).

All sing in their heart and special notes (tonic sofa of peoples choirs) since they made the Romance of Arthur and other legends. Wales is spotted with many castles which Norman King built to see them, but they escaped into its invisible mountains where you can see the grandeur today.

Its mayor is an international *essteidffod* which you cannot translate. It is in a huge camp with chordal singers and fork-dancers who come in their grupps and customs from everywhere to make a big context. You will see in this little town Yugoslavie or Balear or Greeks with their national leggings or they can be in coat and toils and glittered night dresses on the stage to sing the big gems of Palestina or Bach.

It is a shoot-off from their local—each year some where another it is a National *Eisttoddfed* for real (welsh) peoples who practice a traditional typical *penicillin* singing (with a free harp), odes and chorales; the first prize is a Solemn Chaining of the Bard in a ceremony of Druids.

Below, the Menial Strait full of pleasing sails, you can see the island of *Anglesey*. It is with a vast fringe of castles. Chief, at the top are *Conway*, very thick with eight towels, and bottom the most famous is *Carnaervon* a grand disposition of parapels which shine in the water and an Eagle

*The Deputy Arch Druid is passed through a line of Bards (poets)
at Eisteddfod, Wales.*

Tower. It is a ceremonial for the Investment of the Price of Wales.

Soon you will see the splendid wild pears of Snowdon land and other mountains of North Wales; but first you should make an entry in the famous garden of *Bodnant* where you can feast on some bushed terraces of mangolia, camella and a miracle of tuned leafs in its own habitation of scenery.

Snowdon is not an alp but has an optimal proportion to look like them, and you can choose: climb up its rock (it has an Outward Bond Adventure) or you can arise up in a little easy train.

It is all a massive with jammed ranks and stern nodding in its highs but graceful in the low from its sweep sides to some little fishy hotels you can find hidden, also many waters and farms where you can guest with the sheep bloating to the sky in a calm rustic.

South West is called Little England in Wales because the Noresmen pierced it and made a pretty cathedral of *St David* in the national park which cannot be spoiled, also a very handsome bishop's palace with some elegant high arcades of stone (pink).

You cannot pass by a great mixture of steel works with cows and some mines. It is the Valleys, famous Depressions Area and hot bed for some rooted politicals who have made a bit at Westminster Government (Anedrin Bevan, Lloyd Geogre, Michael Foot, Ebbw Vale and some more famous Welsh).

Its indigents are miners but their pit was shut by a Coal Board when they nationalised it, now they make watches, corsets and other light engines in their Valleys; also you must note some passionate feeling in their National Democratic of rugby when they 'scram down' their heads or make a marvellous flying scissors.

Their capital is Cardiff with a fine civic middle of washed tiles and an opera with particular voices in its chorus. Then you can whiz on a marvellous new cabled suspender, the Seven bridge and M6 motorway, back to London; it is the end of your romance in Wales, Land of Sony!

A traditional news paper man.

SOME USEFUL TIPS OF THE TONGUE

In the Shop

(1) I wish a shirt of English broads.

(2) Kindly correct me to the ravers compartment (Carnaby Street).

(3) I have tinkled a bell but it is empty.

(4) Demonstrate me some corsetts in niger, sexe or rust.

(5) Please to forget this, I seemed it was the ticket (price) on the shirt, not the tie only.

(6) I must bespeak a realy-made cloth suit.

At the Garage

(1) I have a puncture. If you cannot, please borrow a john to me and by myself will change the wheel.

(2) But you have three spanners in AA book, kindly make a fast express call to get the sparse part.

(3) You have overed my bill, it was only a plug.

(4) Has the fitting man consumed his tea?

(5) You have spoiled the patrol into my bagage-trunk.

(6) If the mechanical is sick till Tuesday I must have a tired car from you agent.

(7) The screenwipers have ceased to flutter.

On the road

(1) Gentleman! He has bumped the rear when I stopp.

(2) I did a sign on the ladies behind.

At the railway station

(1) Show me a late train from the one before, it will be early for its next.

(2) What time is the next strike?

(3) The signalmann has fainted.

(4) The overhead lines are under.

At the doctors

(1) I am a *bone-fido* visitor. Kindly proscribe me some national spectacles, some teeth and a wag.

At the Post Office

(1) This telephone is out of work, bring me another.

(2) What is the value of a letter stamp this week?

(3) This telephone has availed my money and sounds not.

At the Hotel

(1) Walter! You have done a rubbish of my steak. It is too far.

(2) Is it a compulsion to din before 7?

(3) Walter, bring me a Scotch broth and Yorkshire pudding.

(4) I esteem you have errored the children at a man's price.

(5) Tomorrow, please send me an early tea pot in the chamber, also a journal.

(6) My aunt has drowned in the annex.